MY BIG BLACK HAWK

ALL THE GIRLS LOVE

MY BIG BLACK HAWK

WHEN THEY COME TO RIDE

HE MAKES THEM ALL SQUAWK

BIG BLACK HAWK
HAS A GIANT BLACK HEAD

BIG BLACK HAWK ONLY
SLEEPS IN MY BED

BIG BLACK HAWK
SCARES THE FELLAS

EXCEPT MY FRIEND JACK

BIG BLACK HAWK
MAKES YOU JEALOUS

BECAUSE HE'S SO BLACK

BLACK HAWK IS JACK'S
MOST FAVOURITE RIDE

BUT I CAN'T
GET JACK OFF

UNTIL HE'S SATISFIED

CUCUMBER CURTIS

Can't come to dinner. Your mom has other plans for this innocent little vegetable.

GLUCK GLUCK 3000

Sex Robots are the new wave of the future in sexual entertainment. In fact, they're already in the process of being built. Catering to the needs of lonely men and women, these bots will soon be ubiquitous.

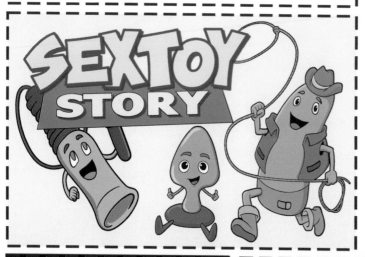

Only $10

RACE WARS

Black, car, white car, and yellow car too.

STD'S & YOU

Learning From The Animals At The Zoo

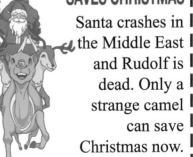

BAA BAA BLACK SHEEP
Deals With Another Routine Stop

Baa baa black sheep please step out of the car. Yes sir yes sir please know I'm unarmed. Do you know why I stopped you today?. "Because of the fur color I display?". You match the description of a suspect I seek. Funny it's the 4th time to happen this week. I profiled you because you are black. And you drive a Mercedes which seems kinda whack.

MOMS ONLYFANS
New Beginnings From Difficult Choices

Dad left your mom broke. Now she's faced with the harsh reality of not having enough money. But don't worry she has a plan to get back on her feet.

CLIP CLOP
The Racist Horse Cop

Does Anyone Know Whatever Happened To MURDER HORNETS

Remember Murder Hornets? Whatever happened to them? We dive deeply into the terror phenomenon that never came to be. 2020 had so many bigger things, so Murder Hornets were forgotten.

Make Your Own Luck

What can pimps and divorce lawyers teach children, about money and luck? This book tells the story of outdated wisdom and harsh truths.

Cockroach-baby smells really musky. Centipede baby was sewn from human skin. Squid-fish lives deep down in the sea. Flesh-eating ladybug is super scary. Bearded baby was born this hairy.

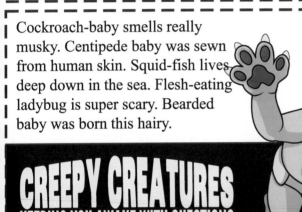

CREEPY CREATURES
KEEPING YOU AWAKE WITH QUESTIONS

SOFA KING

KLUKEE
The Plant Based Chicken

Only $10

OURS BABY
The Only Child Your Step Mom Loves

Your stepmom wants one thing from your dear old dad. Viable sperm and an empty house. Pack your bags it's time to grow up.

MOMMY GOT A DUI

Your mom has secrets. She hides her drinking from you… Until now. Mommy can't drive you to school and you're going to have to learn the bus routes.

INSOMNIAC & FRIENDS
The Clowns That Put You To Sleep

Yeetyeet likes to watch you sleep. Pickles under your bed he creeps. Switchblade eats your favorite stuffies. Pedo lures you away with puppies. Shifty plans to collect your teeth. Twisty smells your hair while you sleep. Clammy lives inside his van. Hank once had to kill a man. Tooty smells your dirty socks. Busby laughs at electric shocks. Twinkles spends the night robbing graves. Fappy keeps a few human slaves.

MY RACIST GRAN

WHY DADDY HITS MOMMY

A Kids Guide To Understanding Alcoholism

DEAD BABIES
COLORING BOOKS

Only $10

OK BOOMER

Boomer always complains at the store. But it was on sale yesterday!! When yesterday's special isn't available anymore. You shouldn't be such a slut. Boomer gives unsolicited advice. This smart phone is dumber than dirt. Boomer always struggles with his device. Boomer demands your supervisor.

DON'T BATHE WITH UNCLE JOE
Setting Boundaries With Adults

Uncle Joe lost his job. For misconduct in the workplace. He's coming to stay with us. You're going to have to learn to avoid his hands and more importantly. NEVER bathe with uncle Joe.

THIRST TRAPS
Why Moms Phone Keeps Blowing Up

DADDY'S A SIMP
Don't Expect Much Inheritance

HUMPTY DUMPTY
Discovers Workplace Misconduct

COLLECT THEM ALL

- [ ] 14 Of The Most Terrible Children's Books: Ever Written
- [ ] 14 of the Most Terrible Children's Books Ever Written: Part 2
- [ ] 14 of the Most Terrible Children's Books Ever Written: Part 3
- [ ] 14 Of The Most Terrible Children's Books: Part 4
- [ ] Clip Clop: The Racist Horse Cop
- [ ] Boo-Cockee: The Rooster That Stalks Me
- [ ] Mom Runs Trains: On the weekend with dad's friends
- [ ] Candi's Nuts: Come in the morning each day
- [ ] Gluck Gluck 3000
- [ ] Gluck Gluck 9000
- [ ] Cucumber Curtis: Can't Come To Dinner
- [ ] Race Wars
- [ ] Cinnamon: A Horse Forced Into The Sex Trade
- [ ] Baa Baa Black Sheep: Deals With Another "Routine" Stop
- [ ] Don't Bathe With Uncle Joe: Setting Boundaries With Adults
- [ ] Dead Babies: A Series Of Short Life Stories
- [ ] Why Daddy Hits Mommy: Kid's Guide To Understanding Alcoholism
- [ ] Dad's a Cuck
- [ ] Mom + Dad + Chad: Your Parents Have Formed a Triad
- [ ] My Racist Gran: Says We Still Can't Trust The Japs
- [ ] How Daddy Got An STD: Understanding Safe Sex And Prostitution
- [ ] Moms Only fans: New Beginnings From Difficult Choices
- [ ] Thirst Traps: Why Mom's Phone Is Always Blowing Up
- [ ] We're Not Camping: Mom And Dad Lied We're Homeless
- [ ] Help Me Step Bro: Creative Prompts For Quality Movies
- [ ] You People: Acceptable Ways To Use That Phrase
- [ ] Daddy's A SIMP: Don't Expect Much Inheritance
- [ ] The Cat That Shat
- [ ] Mommy Got a DUI: A Kid's Guide To Getting Around On The Bus
- [ ] Meet The Karens: They're Angry And They Want Attention
- [ ] Why Mommy Hits Daddy: Kids Guide To Understanding Alcoholism
- [ ] Religion: Controlling people with mythical fear
- [ ] Your Life Is A Lie: Your Parents Created a False Reality
- [ ] Uncle Bob: Can't Wait To Show Me His Knob
- [ ] Sex Toy Story
- [ ] Dead Babies 2: A Series Of Short Life Stories
- [ ] Child Services: They're Coming For You and Your Big Sister Too
- [ ] My Homophobic Dad: Says God Hates Same Sex Couples
- [ ] Humpty Dumpty: Discovers Workplace Misconduct
- [ ] Girls I Stopped Following:: For You
- [ ] STD's & You: Learning From The Animals At The Zoo
- [ ] There Is No Farm: Kids Guide To Understanding Euthanasia
- [ ] Cinnamon: Visits The Glue Factory
- [ ] Coronavirus And Friends: The Outbreak Gang of Killer Sicknesses
- [ ] OK Boomer: It's Not About Age. It's About Attitude
- [ ] Sex Offenders: Trying To Be Good In Your Neighbourhood
- [ ] Insomniac and Friends: The Clowns That Put You To Sleep
- [ ] Things You Should KNow: At This Stage In Your Life
- [ ] Self Isolation: 16 Ways To Prevent Boredom
- [ ] Pedoclown: Can't Catch A Break
- [ ] Furious George: Tears Off Your Mothers Face
- [ ] Triggered: Kids Guide To Modern Day Cancel Culture
- [ ] How Cows Become Burgers: Follow Along From Farm To Table
- [ ] 18 Ways To Tell Kids That Their Parents Died
- [ ] Donkeybear: The Story Of Inbreeding
- [ ] Daddy Daughter Date Night: It's Not What It Seems
- [ ] Sofa King
- [ ] Everything's Tremendous: We're The Best In The World
- [ ] Suppositories: The pills you put in your butt
- [ ] Moms Tinder Profile: And 22 Other Ways Adults Lie Every Day
- [ ] Rich Kids: They're Better Than You
- [ ] Conjoined Twins: So Many Unanswered Questions
- [ ] Make Your Own Luck: Practical Money Advice For Kids
- [ ] Ice Cream Man: Goes Pee In The Back Of His Truck
- [ ] Camel Tony: He Loves Roast Beef and He Hates Pepperoni
- [ ] Dead Babies 3: A Series Of Short Life Stories
- [ ] Mixed Animals: Are Unique Just Like You
- [ ] That's Hot: Kids Guide To What's Hot and What's Not
- [ ] Guys I stopped Following: For You
- [ ] Kluckee: The Plant Based Chicken
- [ ] Santas Lil Humper: Saves Christmas
- [ ] Gender Pronouns: What's The Big Deal?
- [ ] Meet The Hipsters: Ethically Sourced And Sustainable
- [ ] When Parents Go To Jail
- [ ] Cavity Cat: He Comes In Your Mouth And Gives You Cavities
- [ ] Sick Pets: To Make You Sad Before Bed Time
- [ ] Candy Man Van: Strangers Come In All Shapes and Sizes
- [ ] A Is For Alcoholism: Alphabet Soup
- [ ] Conjoined Twins 2: Where Does One End and The Other Begin?
- [ ] Pets In Trouble: What Did They Do Wrong?
- [ ] Creepy Creatures
- [ ] Murder Hornets
- [ ] Ours Baby
- [ ] Why Grandpa Lives In The Garage

Printed in Great Britain
by Amazon

35260073R00016